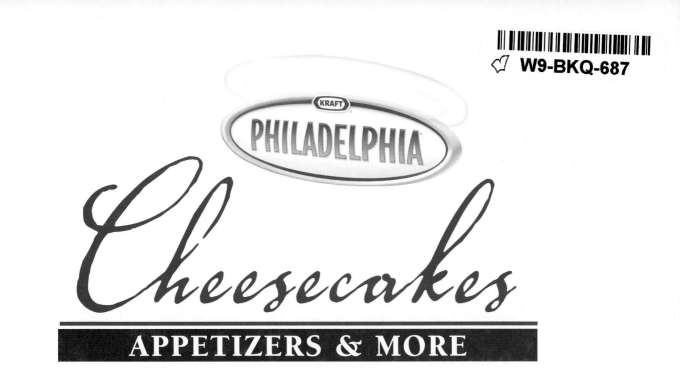

KRAFT

PHILADELPHIA

Cheesecakes

APPETIZERS & MORE

⌐P⌐i⌐L

Publications International, Ltd.
Favorite Brand Name Recipes at www.fbnr.com

PHILADELPHIA, PHILLY, PHILLY 3-STEP, KRAFT, BREAKSTONE'S, KNUDSEN, ATHENOS, OSCAR MAYER, DI GIORNO, COOL WHIP, BAKER'S, JELL-O, MAXWELL HOUSE, ANGEL FLAKE and CALUMET are registered trademarks of Kraft Foods Holdings.

TACO BELL and HOME ORIGINALS are registered trademarks owned and licensed by Taco Bell Corp.

Kraft Kitchens, Sr. Consumer Food Manager: Lori Bowen Tillock, R.D.
Recipe Testing: Lori Hartnett, Mary Jane Laws, Maiko Miyamoto, Wendy Spinelli
Assistant Brand Manager: Deborah Winick
Associate Promotion Manager: Susan Pittner
Assistant Promotion Manager: Lisa Smith

Photography: Peter Walters Photography/Chicago
Photographers: Peter Walters, Kathy Watt
Photographers' Assistants: Eric Coughlin, Chris Lake
Prop Stylist: Sally Grimes
Food Stylists: Lynn Gagné, Carol Parik, Bonnie Rabert
Assistant Food Stylist: Liza Brown, R.D.

Falling snow art designed by: Robin Moro

Pictured on the front cover: PHILADELPHIA® 3-STEP® White Chocolate Raspberry Swirl Cheesecake *(page 70)*.

Pictured on the back cover *(clockwise from top):* Baked Cream Cheese Appetizer *(page 20)*, Café Latte Cheesecake *(page 52)* and Holiday Cheesecake Presents *(page 80)*.

Preparation/Cooking Times: Preparation times are based on the approximate amount of time required to assemble the recipe before cooking, baking, chilling or serving. These times include preparation steps such as measuring, chopping and mixing. The fact that some preparations and cooking can be done simultaneously is taken into account. Preparation of optional ingredients and serving suggestions is not included.

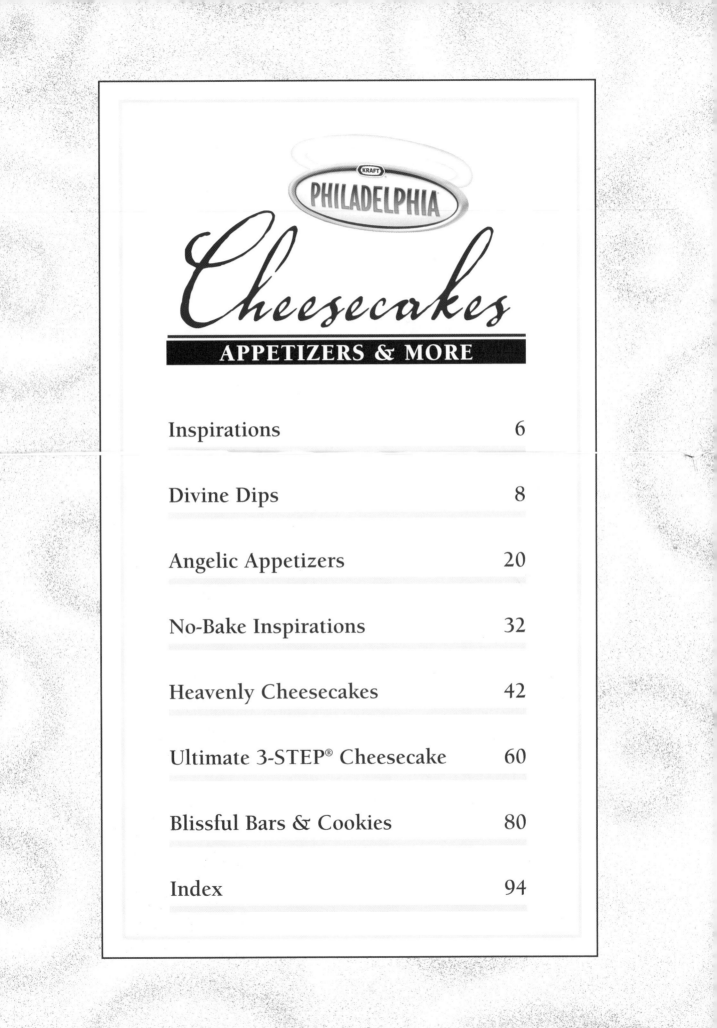

KRAFT
PHILADELPHIA
Cheesecakes
APPETIZERS & MORE

Inspirations

KRAFT
PHILADELPHIA

Tempt your family and friends with
A Little Taste of Heaven®

The holidays are a special time to be enjoyed with family and friends. Whether it's a festive celebration or just a casual get-together, recipes with PHILADELPHIA® cream cheese can help you prepare great food ideas without a hassle so you can kick back and enjoy! In this book, you'll find delicious recipe ideas for easy dips and spreads, simple appetizers, indulgent desserts and irresistible cheesecakes.

Since 1880, the heavenly taste of PHILADELPHIA® cream cheese has been made using only the finest ingredients. The rich, creamy taste of PHILADELPHIA® cream cheese makes every eating experience indulgent. Whether spreading it on bagels and crackers, or using it to create an irresistible recipe, PHILADELPHIA® cream cheese gives all your favorite dishes A Little Taste of Heaven®.

PHILADELPHIA® offers a whole line of sweet and savory flavors in regular, light, and fat free varieties to satisfy every appetite and any occasion.

Indulge in regular PHILADELPHIA® Flavors in Strawberry, Cheesecake, Honey Nut, Pineapple, Chive and Onion, Salmon, and Garden Vegetable.

Let your tastebuds run wild with PHILADELPHIA® Light Flavors, available in Blueberry, Raspberry, Roasted Garlic, Jalapeño, Garden Vegetable, Strawberry, and Chive and Onion.

Help yourself to a truly sinless treat with PHILADELPHIA® FREE in Strawberry.

Tips

For a quick and easy snack, try dipping pretzels, crackers or baby carrots into PHILADELPHIA® Garden Vegetable Cream Cheese.

To satisfy your sweet craving, try spreading PHILADELPHIA® Strawberry Cream Cheese on graham crackers or vanilla wafers.

For more tempting recipes and treats, indulge in our website at **www.creamcheese.com**.

PHILADELPHIA

Divine Dips

Cheesecake Cream Dip

Prep: 5 minutes plus refrigerating

**1 pkg. (8 oz.) PHILADELPHIA Cream Cheese, softened
1 jar (7 oz.) marshmallow cream**

MIX cream cheese and marshmallow cream until well blended.
Refrigerate.

SERVE with assorted cut-up fruit, pound cake or cookies.

Makes 1½ cups

Creamy Pesto Dip

Prep: 5 minutes plus refrigerating

1 pkg. (8 oz.) PHILADELPHIA Cream Cheese, softened
3 Tbsp. milk
⅓ cup DI GIORNO Basil Pesto
1 red pepper, finely chopped (about 1 cup)

MIX cream cheese and milk with electric mixer on medium speed until smooth. Blend in pesto and red pepper. Refrigerate.

SERVE with assorted cut-up vegetables, breadsticks or chips.

Makes about 2⅓ cups

Chili Cheese Dip

Prep: 5 minutes	*Microwave:* 3 minutes

1 pkg. (8 oz.) PHILADELPHIA Cream Cheese, softened
1 can (15 oz.) chili with <u>or</u> without beans
1 cup KRAFT Shredded Cheddar Cheese

SPREAD cream cheese onto bottom and up side of 9-inch microwavable pie plate or quiche dish. Spread chili over cream cheese. Sprinkle with cheddar cheese.

MICROWAVE on HIGH 3 minutes or until thoroughly heated.

SERVE with tortilla chips.

Makes 3 cups

Creamy Pesto Dip

Creamy Roasted Red Pepper Dip

Prep: 5 minutes plus refrigerating

> 1 pkg. (8 oz.) PHILADELPHIA Cream Cheese, softened
> 3 Tbsp. milk
> ½ cup roasted red peppers, drained, chopped
> ½ tsp. dried thyme leaves
> ⅛ tsp. ground black pepper

MIX cream cheese and milk with electric mixer on medium speed until smooth. Blend in remaining ingredients. Refrigerate.

SERVE with assorted cut-up vegetables.   *Makes 1½ cups*

Hot Crab Dip

Prep: 10 minutes   *Bake:* 30 minutes

> 2 pkg. (8 oz. each) PHILADELPHIA Cream Cheese, softened
> 2 cans (6 oz. each) crabmeat, rinsed, drained and flaked
> ½ cup KRAFT Shredded Parmesan Cheese
> ¼ cup chopped green onions
> 2 tsp. KRAFT Prepared Horseradish

MIX all ingredients with electric mixer on medium speed until well blended. Spoon into 9-inch pie plate or quiche dish.

BAKE at 350°F for 25 to 30 minutes or until very lightly browned.

SERVE with crackers.   *Makes 4 cups*

Creamy Roasted Red Pepper Dip

Hot Artichoke Dip

Prep: 15 minutes   *Bake:* 25 minutes

1 pkg. (8 oz.) PHILADELPHIA Cream Cheese, softened
1 can (14 oz.) artichoke hearts, drained, chopped
½ cup KRAFT Mayo Real Mayonnaise
½ cup KRAFT 100% Grated Parmesan Cheese
1 clove garlic, minced

MIX all ingredients with electric mixer on medium speed until well blended. Spoon into 9-inch pie plate or quiche dish.

BAKE at 350°F for 20 to 25 minutes or until very lightly browned.

SERVE with baked pita bread wedges or vegetable dippers.

Makes 2½ cups

Tip

Special Extras: To make baked pita bread wedges, cut each of 3 split pita breads into 8 triangles. Place on cookie sheet. Bake at 350°F for 10 to 12 minutes or until crisp. Makes 48 wedges.

Hot Artichoke Dip

Creamy Salsa Dip

Prep: 10 minutes plus refrigerating

---

1 pkg. (8 oz.) PHILADELPHIA Cream Cheese, softened
1 cup TACO BELL HOME ORIGINALS Salsa

MIX cream cheese and salsa until well blended. Refrigerate.

SERVE with tortilla chips or assorted cut-up vegetables.

Makes 2 cups

Spinach Dip

Prep: 10 minutes plus refrigerating

---

1 pkg. (8 oz.) PHILADELPHIA Cream Cheese, softened
¼ cup milk
1 pkg. (10 oz.) frozen chopped spinach, thawed, drained
1 can (8 oz.) water chestnuts, drained, chopped
½ cup chopped red pepper
½ tsp. garlic salt
⅛ tsp. hot pepper sauce

MIX cream cheese and milk with electric mixer on medium speed until smooth. Blend in remaining ingredients. Refrigerate.

SERVE with assorted cut-up vegetables or potato chips.

Makes 3 cups

Creamy Salsa Dip

7-Layer Mexican Dip

Prep: 10 minutes plus refrigerating

1 pkg. (8 oz.) PHILADELPHIA Cream Cheese, softened
1 Tbsp. TACO BELL HOME ORIGINALS Taco Seasoning Mix
1 cup <u>each</u> guacamole, TACO BELL HOME ORIGINALS
    Salsa and shredded lettuce
1 cup KRAFT Shredded Mild Cheddar Cheese
½ cup chopped green onions
2 Tbsp. sliced pitted ripe olives

MIX cream cheese and seasoning mix. Spread onto bottom of 9-inch pie plate or quiche dish.

LAYER guacamole, salsa, lettuce, cheddar cheese, onions and olives over cream cheese mixture. Refrigerate.

SERVE with tortilla chips.   *Makes 6 to 8 servings*

Tip

Great Substitutes: *If your family doesn't like guacamole, try substituting 1 cup TACO BELL HOME ORIGINALS Refried Beans.*

7-Layer Mexican Dip

PHILADELPHIA

Angelic Appetizers

Baked Cream Cheese Appetizer

Prep: 10 minutes   *Bake:* 18 minutes

> 1 pkg. (4 oz.) refrigerated crescent dinner rolls
> 1 pkg. (8 oz.) PHILADELPHIA Cream Cheese
> ½ tsp. dill weed
> 1 egg white, beaten

UNROLL dough on lightly greased cookie sheet; press seams together to form 12×4-inch rectangle.

SPRINKLE cream cheese with dill; lightly press dill into cream cheese. Place cream cheese, dill-side up, in center of dough. Bring edges of dough up over cream cheese; press edges together to seal, completely enclosing cream cheese. Brush with egg white.

BAKE at 350°F for 15 to 18 minutes or until lightly browned. Serve with crackers, French bread or cut-up vegetables.   *Makes 8 servings*

Party Cheese Wreath

Prep: 15 minutes plus refrigerating

2 pkg. (8 oz. each) PHILADELPHIA Cream Cheese, softened
1 pkg. (8 oz.) KRAFT Shredded Sharp Cheddar Cheese
1 Tbsp. <u>each</u> chopped red bell pepper and finely chopped
   onion
2 tsp. Worcestershire sauce
1 tsp. lemon juice
   Dash ground red pepper

MIX cream cheese and cheddar cheese with electric mixer on medium speed until well blended.

BLEND in remaining ingredients. Refrigerate several hours or overnight.

PLACE drinking glass in center of serving platter. Drop rounded tablespoonfuls of cheese mixture around glass, just touching outer edge of glass to form ring; smooth with spatula. Remove glass. Serve with crackers.   *Makes 12 servings*

Variation

Mini Cheese Balls: *Shape cream cheese mixture into 1-inch balls. Roll in light rye bread crumbs or dark pumpernickel bread crumbs.*

Party Cheese Wreath

Creamy Feta & Sun-Dried Tomato Spread

Prep: 10 minutes plus refrigerating

1 pkg. (8 oz.) PHILADELPHIA Cream Cheese, softened
1 pkg. (4 oz.) ATHENOS Crumbled Feta Cheese
2 Tbsp. chopped fresh basil
2 Tbsp. finely chopped sun-dried tomatoes

MIX all ingredients. Refrigerate.

SERVE with crackers or fresh vegetables.

Makes 1½ cups

Zesty Shrimp Spread

Prep: 5 minutes plus refrigerating

1 pkg. (8 oz.) PHILADELPHIA Cream Cheese, softened
½ cup KRAFT Mayo Real Mayonnaise
1 cup chopped, cooked, cleaned shrimp
¼ cup KRAFT 100% Grated Parmesan Cheese
2 Tbsp. chopped fresh parsley <u>or</u> cilantro
2 cloves garlic, minced

BEAT cream cheese and mayo with electric mixer on medium speed until well blended.

ADD remaining ingredients; mix well. Refrigerate.

SERVE with crackers or toasted bread rounds.

Makes 2¼ cups

Creamy Feta & Sun-Dried Tomato Spread

Bacon Appetizer Crescents

Prep: 30 minutes	*Bake:* 15 minutes

> 1 pkg. (8 oz.) PHILADELPHIA Cream Cheese, softened
> ½ cup OSCAR MAYER Bacon Bits <u>or</u> 8 slices OSCAR MAYER
>   Bacon, crisply cooked, crumbled
> ⅓ cup KRAFT 100% Grated Parmesan Cheese
> ¼ cup thinly sliced green onions
> 1 Tbsp. milk
> 2 cans (8 oz. each) refrigerated crescent dinner rolls
>   Poppy seeds (optional)

MIX cream cheese, bacon bits, Parmesan cheese, onions and milk until well blended.

SEPARATE dough into 8 rectangles; firmly press perforations together to seal. Spread each rectangle with 2 rounded tablespoonfuls cream cheese mixture.

CUT each rectangle in half diagonally; repeat with opposite corners. Cut in half crosswise to form 6 triangles. Roll up triangles, starting at short ends. Place, point sides down, on ungreased cookie sheets. Sprinkle with poppy seeds.

BAKE at 375°F for 12 to 15 minutes or until golden brown. Serve immediately.   *Makes 4 dozen*

Savory Cheese Ball

Prep: 10 minutes plus refrigerating

1 pkg. (8 oz.) PHILADELPHIA Cream Cheese, softened
1 pkg. (8 oz.) KRAFT Shredded Sharp Cheddar Cheese
¾ cup crumbled KRAFT Blue Cheese
¼ cup chopped green onions
2 Tbsp. milk
1 tsp. Worcestershire sauce
   Finely chopped walnuts

MIX cheeses, green onions, milk and Worcestershire sauce until well blended. Refrigerate 1 to 2 hours.

SHAPE into ball; roll in walnuts. Serve with apple and pear slices.

Makes 2⅔ cups

Tip

Great Substitutes: *Substitute finely chopped pecans or almonds for walnuts.*

Three Pepper Quesadillas

Prep: 20 minutes	*Bake:* 8 minutes

> 1 cup <u>each</u> thin green, red and yellow pepper strips
> ½ cup thin onion slices
> ½ tsp. ground cumin
> ⅓ cup butter <u>or</u> margarine
> 1 pkg. (8 oz.) PHILADELPHIA Cream Cheese, softened
> 1 pkg. (8 oz.) KRAFT Shredded Sharp Cheddar Cheese
> 10 flour tortillas (6 inch)
> TACO BELL HOME ORIGINALS Salsa

COOK and stir peppers, onion and cumin in butter in large skillet 4 minutes or until vegetables are tender-crisp. Drain, reserving butter.

MIX cream cheese and cheddar cheese until well blended. Spoon 2 Tbsp. cheese mixture onto each tortilla; top with scant ⅓ cup vegetable mixture. Fold tortillas in half; place on cookie sheet. Brush with reserved butter.

BAKE at 425°F for 8 minutes. Cut each tortilla into thirds. Serve warm with salsa.   *Makes 30 appetizers*

Three Pepper Quesadillas

Pesto Christmas Tree

Prep: 5 minutes

> 1 pkg. (8 oz.) PHILADELPHIA Cream Cheese
> ⅓ cup DI GIORNO Pesto
>   Cinnamon stick

CUT cream cheese in half diagonally. Place triangles together to form Christmas tree shape on serving plate.

TOP with pesto. Insert cinnamon stick at base of triangle for "tree trunk." Serve with crackers.   *Makes 12 servings*

Tip

Special Extras: *Use chopped red bell pepper as "ornaments" to decorate tree.*

Pesto Christmas Tree

No-Bake *Inspirations*

Cherries in the Snow

Prep: 10 minutes

---

1 pkg. (8 oz.) PHILADELPHIA Cream Cheese, softened
½ cup sugar
2 cups thawed COOL WHIP Whipped Topping
1 can (20 oz.) cherry pie filling, divided

MIX cream cheese and sugar in large bowl until smooth. Gently stir in whipped topping.

LAYER ¼ cup cream cheese mixture and 2 Tbsp. pie filling in each of 4 dessert bowls. Repeat layers.   *Makes 4 servings*

Chocolate Truffles

Prep: 20 minutes plus refrigerating

3 cups sifted powdered sugar
1 pkg. (8 oz.) PHILADELPHIA Cream Cheese, softened
1 pkg. (12 oz.) BAKER'S Semi-Sweet Real Chocolate Chips,
   melted
1 Tbsp. coffee-flavored liqueur
1 Tbsp. orange-flavored liqueur
1 Tbsp. almond-flavored liqueur
   Ground nuts, powdered sugar, nonpareils or unsweetened
   cocoa

ADD 3 cups powdered sugar gradually to cream cheese, beating with electric mixer on medium speed until well blended. Add melted chocolate; mix well.

DIVIDE mixture into thirds. Add different flavor liqueur to each third; mix well. Refrigerate several hours.

SHAPE mixture into 1-inch balls. Roll in nuts, sugar, nonpareils or cocoa. Refrigerate. *Makes 5 dozen*

Tip

Great Substitutes: *Three or four drops of almond
and orange extracts may be substituted for the liqueur;
use 1 tsp. very strong coffee in place of coffee liqueur.*

Chocolate Truffles

Cappuccino Cream

Prep: 20 minutes plus refrigerating

> 1 pkg. (8 oz.) PHILADELPHIA Cream Cheese, softened
> 1 cup brewed strong MAXWELL HOUSE Coffee, at room
>   temperature
> ½ cup milk
> 1 pkg. (4-serving size) JELL-O Brand Vanilla Flavor Instant
>   Pudding & Pie Filling
> ¼ tsp. ground cinnamon
> 1 tub (8 oz.) COOL WHIP Whipped Topping, thawed,
>   divided
>   Cookies, such as chocolate-laced pirouettes <u>or</u> biscotti

MIX cream cheese with electric mixer on medium speed until smooth. Gradually add coffee and milk, beating until well blended. Add pudding mix and cinnamon. Beat on low speed 2 minutes. Let stand 5 minutes or until thickened.

STIR in 2 cups of the whipped topping. Spoon mixture into 6 dessert glasses or 1-quart serving bowl.

REFRIGERATE until ready to serve. Just before serving, top with remaining whipped topping. Serve with cookies.

Makes 6 servings

Cappuccino Cream

36

Fluffy 2-Step Cheesecake

Prep: 15 minutes plus refrigerating

> 2 pkg. (8 oz. each) PHILADELPHIA Cream Cheese, softened
> $\frac{1}{3}$ cup sugar
> 1 tub (8 oz.) COOL WHIP Whipped Topping, thawed
> 1 ready-to-use graham cracker crumb crust (6 oz. or 9 inch)

MIX cream cheese and sugar in large bowl with electric mixer on medium speed until smooth. Gently stir in whipped topping.

SPOON into crust. Refrigerate 3 hours or until set. Top with fresh fruit or cherry pie filling, if desired. Store leftover cheesecake in refrigerator.

Makes 8 servings

Chocolate Fudge

Prep: 15 minutes plus refrigerating

> 4 cups sifted powdered sugar
> 1 pkg. (8 oz.) PHILADELPHIA Cream Cheese, softened
> 4 squares BAKER'S Unsweetened Baking Chocolate, melted
> $\frac{1}{2}$ cup chopped nuts
> 1 tsp. vanilla

ADD sugar gradually to cream cheese, beating with electric mixer on medium speed until well blended. Mix in remaining ingredients.

SPREAD into greased 8-inch square pan. Refrigerate several hours.

CUT into 1-inch squares. Refrigerate leftover fudge.

Makes 64 squares

Fluffy 2-Step Cheesecake

Easy English Trifle

Prep: 15 minutes plus refrigerating

> 1 pkg. (8 oz.) PHILADELPHIA Cream Cheese, softened
> 2 cups milk, divided
> 1 pkg. (4-serving size) JELL-O Vanilla Flavor Instant Pudding
>   & Pie Filling
> 2½ cups cubed pound cake
> ½ cup strawberry preserves
> 1 can (16 oz.) peach slices, drained, chopped

MIX cream cheese and ½ cup of the milk with electric mixer on medium speed until well blended. Add pudding mix and remaining 1½ cups milk; beat on low speed 1 minute.

LAYER ½ each of the cake, preserves, peach slices and pudding mixture in 1½-quart serving bowl; repeat layers. Cover surface with wax paper or plastic wrap; refrigerate.   *Makes 8 servings*

Chocolate Raspberry Cheesecake

Prep: 10 minutes plus refrigerating

> ½ cup raspberry fruit spread
> 1 ready-to-use graham cracker crumb crust (6 oz. or 9 inch)
> 2 pkg. (8 oz. each) PHILADELPHIA Cream Cheese, softened
> 1¼ cups chocolate flavored dessert topping
> 1 tub (8 oz.) COOL WHIP Whipped Topping, thawed

SPREAD fruit spread onto bottom of crust.

MIX cream cheese and dessert topping with electric mixer on medium speed until smooth. Gently stir in whipped topping.

SPOON over fruit spread in crust. Refrigerate 3 hours or until set. Drizzle with additional dessert topping, if desired.   *Makes 8 servings*

Easy English Trifle

Brownie Bottom Cheesecake

Prep: 20 minutes plus refrigerating	*Bake:* 65 minutes

1 pkg. (10 to 16 oz.) brownie mix, any variety (8×8-inch pan size)
3 pkg. (8 oz. each) PHILADELPHIA Cream Cheese, softened
¾ cup sugar
1 tsp. vanilla
½ cup BREAKSTONE'S or KNUDSEN Sour Cream
3 eggs

PREPARE and bake brownie mix as directed on package for 8-inch square pan in well-greased 9-inch springform pan.

MIX cream cheese, sugar and vanilla with electric mixer on medium speed until well blended. Blend in sour cream. Add eggs, mixing on low speed just until blended. Pour over brownie crust.

BAKE at 325°F for 60 to 65 minutes or until center is almost set if using a silver springform pan. (Bake at 300°F for 60 to 65 minutes or until center is almost set if using a dark nonstick springform pan.) Run knife or metal spatula around rim of pan to loosen cake; cool before removing rim of pan. Refrigerate 4 hours or overnight.

Makes 12 servings

Classic New York Cheesecake

Prep: 15 minutes plus refrigerating   *Bake:* 70 minutes

Crust
   1 cup graham cracker crumbs
   3 Tbsp. sugar
   3 Tbsp. butter <u>or</u> margarine, melted

Filling
   4 pkg. (8 oz. each) PHILADELPHIA Cream Cheese, softened
   1 cup sugar
   3 Tbsp. flour
   1 Tbsp. vanilla
   1 cup BREAKSTONE'S <u>or</u> KNUDSEN Sour Cream
   4 eggs

Crust
MIX crumbs, sugar and butter; press onto bottom of 9-inch springform pan. Bake at 325°F for 10 minutes if using a silver springform pan. (Bake at 300°F for 10 minutes if using a dark nonstick springform pan.)

Filling
MIX cream cheese, sugar, flour and vanilla with electric mixer on medium speed until well blended. Blend in sour cream. Add eggs, mixing on low speed just until blended. Pour over crust.

BAKE at 325°F for 65 to 70 minutes or until center is almost set if using a 9-inch silver springform pan. (Bake at 300°F for 65 to 70 minutes or until center is almost set if using a 9-inch dark nonstick springform pan.) Run knife or metal spatula around rim of pan to loosen cake; cool before removing rim of pan. Refrigerate 4 hours or overnight.

Makes 12 servings

Classic New York Cheesecake

Tips from the Kraft Kitchens

For great cheesecakes, follow these quick mixing and baking tips:

Mixing:

- Soften PHILADELPHIA Cream Cheese before mixing. To soften in microwave, place an unwrapped (8 oz.) pkg. in microwavable bowl. Microwave on HIGH 15 seconds. Add 15 seconds for each additional package.

- Don't overbeat. Beat at low speed after adding eggs, just until blended.

Baking:

- Don't peek into the oven during baking.

- Don't overbake. When done, edges should be slightly puffed. The center area, about the size of a silver dollar, should still appear soft and moist. The center will firm upon cooling.

Cooling:

- Cool cheesecake on wire rack at room temperature for 1 hour before refrigerating.

- Refrigerate, uncovered, 3 to 4 hours or until thoroughly chilled. Place sheet of plastic wrap or foil over top of cheesecake; secure. Refrigerate overnight or up to 2 days.

Freezing:

- Prepare cheesecake as directed, omitting any topping. Wrap securely in plastic wrap; overwrap with foil. Place in plastic bag and seal. Freeze up to 2 months.

- Thaw wrapped cheesecake in refrigerator overnight.

Easy Steps Toward Success:

Crust:

- For baked springform pan cheesecakes, prepare crust by pressing crust mixture into pan. A mixture of graham cracker crumbs, sugar and melted butter or margarine is shown here.

Loosening Cheesecake from Pan:

- Immediately upon removal from oven, run a thin metal spatula or knife around edge of cheesecake (pushing against side of pan) to loosen it from side of pan. Keep spring fastener on side of pan locked and springform side on. Cool 1 hour at room temperature; refrigerate.

Removing Pan:

- Loosen spring fastener. Lift rim of pan straight up to separate it from cheesecake.

Double Lemon Cheesecake

Prep: 35 minutes plus refrigerating   *Bake:* 55 minutes

Crust
   1 cup vanilla wafer cookie crumbs
   3 Tbsp. sugar
   3 Tbsp. butter <u>or</u> margarine, melted

Filling
   3 pkg. (8 oz. each) PHILADELPHIA Cream Cheese, softened
   1 cup sugar
   3 Tbsp. flour
   2 Tbsp. lemon juice
   1 Tbsp. grated lemon peel
   ½ tsp. vanilla
   3 eggs
   1 egg white

Topping
   ¾ cup sugar
   2 Tbsp. cornstarch
   ½ cup water
   ¼ cup lemon juice
   1 egg yolk, beaten

Crust
MIX crumbs, sugar and butter; press onto bottom of 9-inch springform pan. Bake at 325°F for 10 minutes if using a silver springform pan. (Bake at 300°F for 10 minutes if using a dark nonstick springform pan).

Filling
MIX cream cheese, sugar, flour, juice, peel and vanilla with electric mixer on medium speed until well blended. Add 3 eggs and egg white, mixing on low speed just until blended. Pour over crust.

Continued on page 50

Double Lemon Cheesecake

48

Double Lemon Cheesecake, continued

BAKE at 325°F for 50 to 55 minutes or until center is almost set if using a silver springform pan. (Bake at 300°F for 50 to 55 minutes or until center is almost set if using a dark nonstick springform pan). Run knife or metal spatula around rim of pan to loosen cake; cool before removing rim of pan. Refrigerate 4 hours or overnight.

Topping

MIX sugar and cornstarch in saucepan; gradually stir in water and juice. Bring mixture to low boil on medium heat, stirring constantly until clear and thickened. Stir 2 tablespoons of the hot mixture into egg yolks; return to hot mixture. Cook 1 minute or until thickened, stirring constantly. Cool slightly. Spoon topping over cheesecake; refrigerate. *Makes 12 servings*

Tip

Great Substitutes: *You can substitute 1 jar of prepared lemon curd from a specialty food store for lemon topping.*

Amaretto Macaroon Cheesecake

Prep: 25 minutes plus refrigerating   *Bake:* 1 hour

Crust
   1 pkg. (7 oz.) BAKER'S ANGEL FLAKE Coconut, lightly toasted
   ½ cup finely chopped lightly toasted almonds
   1 can (14 oz.) sweetened condensed milk, divided
   ⅓ cup flour
   ¼ cup (½ stick) butter <u>or</u> margarine, melted

Filling
   4 pkg. (8 oz. each) PHILADELPHIA Cream Cheese, softened
   ¼ cup sugar
   ¼ cup almond-flavored liqueur
   4 eggs

Crust
MIX coconut, almonds, ½ cup of the sweetened condensed milk, flour and butter; press onto bottom of greased 9-inch springform pan.

Filling
MIX cream cheese, sugar and remaining ¾ cup sweetened condensed milk with electric mixer on medium speed until well blended. Blend in liqueur. Add eggs, mixing on low speed just until blended. Pour over crust.

BAKE at 325°F for 55 to 60 minutes or until center is almost set if using a silver springform pan. (Bake at 300°F for 55 to 60 minutes or until center is almost set if using a dark nonstick springform pan.) Run knife or metal spatula around rim of pan to loosen cake; cool before removing rim of pan. Refrigerate 4 hours or overnight.

Makes 12 servings

Café Latte Cheesecake

Prep: 25 minutes plus refrigerating	*Bake:* 65 minutes

Crust
- 1 cup vanilla wafer cookie crumbs
- 3 Tbsp. sugar
- 3 Tbsp. butter <u>or</u> margarine, melted

Filling
- 4 pkg. (8 oz. each) PHILADELPHIA Cream Cheese, softened
- 1 cup sugar
- 1 Tbsp. vanilla
- 4 eggs
- 3 Tbsp. milk
- 3 Tbsp. MAXWELL HOUSE Instant Coffee
- 1 Tbsp. warm water

Crust

MIX crumbs, sugar and butter; press onto bottom of 9-inch springform pan. Bake at 325°F for 10 minutes if using a silver springform pan. (Bake at 300°F for 10 minutes if using a dark nonstick springform pan.)

Filling

MIX cream cheese, sugar and vanilla with electric mixer on medium speed until well blended. Add eggs, mixing on low speed just until blended. Reserve 1½ cups of the batter. Stir instant coffee into warm water until dissolved. Add to remaining batter; mix well. Pour over crust. Stir milk into reserved batter; pour gently over coffee batter.

BAKE at 325°F for 65 minutes or until center is almost set if using a sliver springform pan. (Bake at 300°F for 65 minutes or until center is almost set if using a dark nonstick springform pan.) Run knife or metal spatula around rim of pant to loosen cake; cool before removing rim of pan. Refrigerate 4 hours or overnight.

Makes 12 servings

Café Latte Cheesecake

Chocolate Mint Swirl Cheesecake

Prep: 25 minutes plus refrigerating   *Bake:* 1 hour

Crust
   1 cup chocolate wafer cookie crumbs
   3 Tbsp. sugar
   3 Tbsp. butter <u>or</u> margarine, melted

Filling
   4 pkg. (8 oz. each) PHILADELPHIA Cream Cheese, softened
   1 cup sugar
   1 tsp. vanilla
   4 eggs
   2 squares BAKER'S Semi-Sweet Baking Chocolate, melted
   1 pkg. (4.67 oz.) crème de menthe candies, coarsely chopped
   10 drops green food coloring

Crust
MIX crumbs, sugar and butter; press onto bottom of 9-inch springform pan. Bake at 325°F for 10 minutes if using a silver springform pan. (Bake at 300°F for 10 minutes if using a dark nonstick springform pan.)

Filling
MIX cream cheese, sugar and vanilla with electric mixer on medium speed until well blended. Add eggs, mixing on low speed just until blended. Spoon 1½ cups batter into small bowl; blend in melted chocolate. Add mint candies and food coloring to remaining batter. Pour ½ of the mint batter over crust. Using tablespoon, dollop ½ of the chocolate batter over mint batter layer; repeat layers. Cut through batter with knife several times to create marble effect.

BAKE at 325°F for 1 hour or until center is almost set if using a silver springform pan. (Bake at 300°F for 1 hour or until center is almost set if using a dark nonstick springform pan.) Run knife or metal spatula around rim of pan to loosen cake; cool before removing rim of pan. Refrigerate 4 hours or overnight.   *Makes 12 servings*

Chocolate Mint Swirl Cheesecake

Citrus Fruit Cheesecake

Prep: 20 minutes plus refrigerating   *Bake:* 65 minutes

Crust
  1 cup graham cracker crumbs
  ⅓ cup firmly packed brown sugar
  ¼ cup (½ stick) butter <u>or</u> margarine, melted

Filling
  4 pkg. (8 oz. each) PHILADELPHIA Cream Cheese, softened
  1 cup granulated sugar
  2 Tbsp. flour
  1 tsp. vanilla
  1 Tbsp. <u>each</u> fresh lemon juice, lime juice and orange juice
  ½ tsp. <u>each</u> grated lemon peel, lime peel and orange peel
  4 eggs

Crust

MIX crumbs, brown sugar and butter; press onto bottom of 9-inch springform pan. Bake at 325°F for 10 minutes if using a silver springform pan. (Bake at 300°F for 10 minutes if using a dark nonstick springform pan.)

Filling

MIX cream cheese, granulated sugar, flour and vanilla with electric mixer on medium speed until well blended. Blend in juices and peels. Add eggs, mixing on low speed just until blended. Pour over crust.

BAKE at 325°F for 65 minutes or until center is almost set if using a silver springform pan. (Bake at 300°F for 65 minutes or until center is almost set if using a dark nonstick springform pan.) Run knife or metal spatula around rim of pan to loosen cake; cool before removing rim of pan. Refrigerate 4 hours or overnight.

Makes 12 servings

Chocolate Truffle Cheesecake

Prep: 30 minutes plus refrigerating   *Bake:* 1 hour

Crust
1½ cups crushed chocolate sandwich cookies (about
        18 cookies)
  2 Tbsp. butter <u>or</u> margarine, melted

Filling
    3 pkg. (8 oz. each) PHILADELPHIA Cream Cheese, softened
    1 cup sugar
    1 tsp. vanilla
    8 squares BAKER'S Semi-Sweet Baking Chocolate, melted,
        slightly cooled
  ¼ cup hazelnut liqueur (optional)
    3 eggs

Crust
MIX crumbs and butter; press onto bottom of 9-inch springform pan.
Bake at 325°F for 10 minutes if using a silver springform pan. (Bake
at 300°F for 10 minutes if using a dark nonstick springform pan.)

Filling
MIX cream cheese, sugar and vanilla with electric mixer on medium
speed until well blended. Blend in melted chocolate and liqueur. Add
eggs, mixing on low speed just until blended. Pour over crust.

BAKE at 325°F for 55 to 60 minutes or until center is almost set if
using a silver springform pan. (Bake at 300°F for 55 to 60 minutes or
until center is almost set if using a dark nonstick springform pan.)
Run knife or metal spatula around rim of pan to loosen cake; cool
before removing rim of pan. Refrigerate 4 hours or overnight.

Makes 12 servings

Pumpkin Marble Cheesecake

Prep: 25 minutes plus refrigerating	*Bake:* 55 minutes

Crust
   2 cups gingersnap cookie crumbs
   ½ cup finely chopped pecans
   6 Tbsp. butter <u>or</u> margarine, melted

Filling
   3 pkg. (8 oz. each) PHILADELPHIA Cream Cheese, softened
   1 cup sugar, divided
   1 tsp. vanilla
   3 eggs
   1 cup canned pumpkin
   1 tsp. ground cinnamon
   ¼ tsp. ground nutmeg
      Dash ground cloves

Crust
MIX crumbs, pecans and butter; press onto bottom and 2 inches up side of 9-inch springform pan.

Filling
MIX cream cheese, ¾ cup of the sugar and vanilla with electric mixer on medium speed until well blended. Add eggs, mixing on low speed just until blended. Reserve 1½ cups batter. Add remaining ¼ cup sugar, pumpkin and spices to remaining batter; mix well. Spoon ½ of the pumpkin batter over crust; top with spoonfuls of plain batter. Repeat layers. Cut through batter with knife several times for marble effect.

BAKE at 325°F for 55 minutes or until center is almost set if using a silver springform pan. (Bake at 300°F for 55 minutes or until center is almost set if using a dark nonstick springform pan.) Run knife or metal spatula around rim of pan to loosen cake; cool before removing rim of pan. Refrigerate 4 hours or overnight.   *Makes 12 servings*

Pumpkin Marble Cheesecake

PHILADELPHIA® 3-STEP® Cheesecake

Prep: 10 minutes plus refrigerating   *Bake:* 40 minutes

> 2 pkg. (8 oz. each) PHILADELPHIA Cream Cheese, softened
> ½ cup sugar
> ½ tsp. vanilla
> 2 eggs
> 1 ready-to-use graham cracker crumb crust (6 oz. or 9 inch)

MIX cream cheese, sugar and vanilla with electric mixer on medium speed until well blended. Add eggs; mix until blended.

POUR into crust.

BAKE at 350°F for 40 minutes or until center is almost set. Cool. Refrigerate 3 hours or overnight.   *Makes 8 servings*

PHILADELPHIA® 3-STEP® Lime Cheesecake

Prep: 10 minutes plus refrigerating   *Bake:* 40 minutes

> 2 pkg. (8 oz. each) PHILADELPHIA Cream Cheese, softened
> ½ cup sugar
> 2 Tbsp. fresh lime juice
> 1 tsp. grated lime peel
> ½ tsp. vanilla
> 2 eggs
> 1 ready-to-use graham cracker crust (6 oz. or 9 inch)

MIX cream cheese, sugar, juice, peel and vanilla with electric mixer on medium speed until well blended. Add eggs; mix until blended.

POUR into crust.

BAKE at 350°F for 35 to 40 minutes or until center is almost set. Cool. Refrigerate 3 hours or overnight.   *Makes 8 servings*

Variation

Lemon Cheesecake: *Prepare as directed, substituting 1 Tbsp. fresh lemon juice for lime juice and ½ tsp. grated lemon peel for lime peel.*

PHILADELPHIA® 3-STEP® Lime Cheesecake

PHILADELPHIA® 3-STEP® Chocolate Swirl Cheesecake

Prep: 10 minutes plus refrigerating	*Bake:* 40 minutes

> 2 pkg. (8 oz. each) PHILADELPHIA Cream Cheese, softened
> ½ cup sugar
> ½ tsp. vanilla
> 2 eggs
> 1 square BAKER'S Semi-Sweet Baking Chocolate, melted, slightly cooled
> 1 ready-to-use chocolate flavor crumb crust (6 oz. or 9 inch)

MIX cream cheese, sugar and vanilla with electric mixer on medium speed until well blended. Add eggs; mix until blended. Stir melted chocolate into ¾ cup of the cream cheese batter.

POUR remaining cream cheese batter into crust. Spoon chocolate batter over cream cheese batter; cut through batter with knife several times for marble effect.

BAKE at 350°F for 35 to 40 minutes or until center is almost set. Cool. Refrigerate 3 hours or overnight.   *Makes 8 servings*

PHILADELPHIA® 3-STEP® Amaretto Berry Cheesecake

Prep: 10 minutes plus refrigerating   *Bake:* 40 minutes

 2 pkg. (8 oz. each) PHILADELPHIA Cream Cheese, softened
½ cup sugar
½ tsp. vanilla
 2 eggs
 3 Tbsp. almond-flavored liqueur
 1 ready-to-use graham cracker crumb crust (6 oz. or 9 inch)
 2 cups blueberries, raspberries and sliced strawberries

MIX cream cheese, sugar and vanilla with electric mixer on medium speed until well blended. Add eggs; mix until blended. Stir in liqueur.

POUR into crust.

BAKE at 350°F for 35 to 40 minutes or until center is almost set. Cool. Refrigerate 3 hours or overnight. Top with fruit just before serving.
Makes 8 servings

Tip

Great Substitutes: *Try substituting 1 tsp. almond extract for the almond-flavored liqueur.*

PHILADELPHIA® 3-STEP® Mini Cheesecakes

Prep: 10 minutes plus refrigerating   *Bake:* 20 minutes

---

  2 pkg. (8 oz. each) PHILADELPHIA Cream Cheese, softened
½ cup sugar
½ tsp. vanilla
  2 eggs
12 vanilla wafer <u>or</u> chocolate sandwich cookies

MIX cream cheese, sugar and vanilla with electric mixer on medium speed until well blended. Add eggs; mix until blended.

PLACE 1 cookie on bottom of each of 12 paper-lined muffin cups. Pour batter evenly into muffin cups.

BAKE at 350°F for 20 minutes or until centers are almost set. Cool. Refrigerate 3 hours or overnight. Garnish with fresh fruit.

Makes 12 servings

PHILADELPHIA® 3-STEP® Caramel Pecan Cheesecake

Prep: 15 minutes plus refrigerating	*Bake:* 40 minutes

20 caramels
3 Tbsp. milk
½ cup chopped pecans
1 ready-to-use graham cracker crumb crust (6 oz. or 9 inch)
2 pkg. (8 oz. each) PHILADELPHIA Cream Cheese, softened
½ cup sugar
½ tsp. vanilla
2 eggs

MICROWAVE caramels and milk in small bowl on HIGH 2 minutes or until smooth, stirring every minute. Stir in pecans; pour into crust. Refrigerate 10 minutes.

MIX cream cheese, sugar and vanilla with electric mixer on medium speed until well blended. Add eggs; mix until blended. Pour over caramel mixture.

BAKE at 350°F for 35 to 40 minutes or until center is almost set. Cool. Refrigerate 3 hours or overnight. Garnish with pecan halves and caramel sauce.

Makes 8 servings

PHILADELPHIA® 3-STEP® Caramel Pecan Cheesecake

PHILADELPHIA® 3-STEP® White Chocolate Raspberry Swirl Cheesecake

Prep: 10 minutes plus refrigerating	*Bake:* 40 minutes

2 pkg. (8 oz. each) PHILADELPHIA Cream Cheese, softened
½ cup sugar
½ tsp. vanilla
2 eggs
3 squares (3 oz.) BAKER'S Premium White Baking
    Chocolate, melted
1 ready-to-use chocolate flavor crumb crust (6 oz. or 9 inch)
3 Tbsp. red raspberry preserves

MIX cream cheese, sugar and vanilla with electric mixer on medium speed until well blended. Add eggs; mix until blended. Stir in white chocolate.

POUR into crust. Microwave preserves in small bowl on HIGH 15 seconds or until melted. Dot top of cheesecake with small spoonfuls of preserves. Cut through batter with knife several times for swirl effect.

BAKE at 350°F for 35 to 40 minutes or until center is almost set. Cool. Refrigerate 3 hours or overnight.   *Makes 8 servings*

PHILADELPHIA® 3-STEP® Triple Chocolate Layer Cheesecake

Prep: 10 minutes plus refrigerating	*Bake:* 40 minutes

> 2 pkg. (8 oz. each) PHILADELPHIA Cream Cheese, softened
> ½ cup sugar
> ½ tsp. vanilla
> 2 eggs
> 3 squares BAKER'S Semi-Sweet Baking Chocolate, melted, slightly cooled
> 4 squares BAKER'S Premium White Baking Chocolate, melted, slightly cooled
> 1 ready-to-use chocolate flavor crumb crust (6 oz. or 9 inch)

MIX cream cheese, sugar and vanilla with electric mixer on medium speed until well blended. Add eggs; mix until blended. Stir melted semi-sweet chocolate into 1 cup of the batter. Stir melted white chocolate into remaining plain batter.

POUR semi-sweet chocolate batter into crust. Top with white chocolate batter.

BAKE at 350°F for 35 to 40 minutes or until center is almost set. Cool. Refrigerate 3 hours or overnight. *Makes 8 servings*

PHILADELPHIA® 3-STEP® Cappuccino Cheesecake

Prep: 10 minutes plus refrigerating   *Bake:* 40 minutes

---

2 pkg. (8 oz. each) PHILADELPHIA Cream Cheese, softened
½ cup sugar
½ tsp. vanilla
2 eggs
1 Tbsp. milk
2 Tbsp. MAXWELL HOUSE Instant Coffee
1 ready-to-use chocolate crumb crust (6 oz. or 9 inch)

MIX cream cheese, sugar and vanilla with electric mixer on medium speed until well blended. Add eggs; mix until blended.

MICROWAVE milk on HIGH 15 seconds. Stir instant coffee into milk until dissolved. Stir into batter. Pour into crust.

BAKE at 350°F for 35 to 40 minutes or until center is almost set. Cool. Refrigerate 3 hours or overnight.   *Makes 8 servings*

Tip

Special Extras: *When serving cheesecake, wipe knife blade with a damp cloth between each slice for clean edges.*

PHILADELPHIA® 3-STEP® Chocolate Lover's Cheesecake

Prep: 10 minutes plus refrigerating   *Bake:* 40 minutes

> 2 pkg. (8 oz. each) PHILADELPHIA Cream Cheese, softened
> ½ cup sugar
> ½ tsp. vanilla
> 2 eggs
> 4 squares BAKER'S Semi-Sweet Baking Chocolate, melted, slightly cooled
> 1 ready-to-use chocolate flavor crumb crust (6 oz. or 9 inch)

MIX cream cheese, sugar and vanilla at medium speed with electric mixer until well blended. Add eggs; mix until blended. Stir in melted chocolate.

POUR into crust.

BAKE at 350°F for 35 to 40 minutes or until center is almost set. Cool. Garnish with fresh fruit. Refrigerate 3 hours or overnight.

Makes 8 servings

PHILADELPHIA® 3-STEP® Black Forest Cherry Cheesecake

Prep: 10 minutes plus refrigerating	*Bake:* 40 minutes

> 2 pkg. (8 oz. each) PHILADELPHIA Cream Cheese, softened
> ½ cup sugar
> ½ tsp. vanilla
> 2 eggs
> 4 squares BAKER'S Semi-Sweet Baking Chocolate, melted, slightly cooled
> 1 ready-to-use chocolate flavor crumb crust (6 oz. or 9 inch)
> 1 cup thawed COOL WHIP Whipped Topping
> 1 cup cherry pie filling

MIX cream cheese, sugar and vanilla with electric mixer on medium speed until well blended. Add eggs; mix until blended. Stir in melted chocolate.

POUR into crust.

BAKE at 350°F for 35 to 40 minutes or until center is almost set. Cool. Refrigerate 3 hours or overnight. Spread whipped topping over chilled cheesecake; cover with pie filling.   *Makes 8 servings*

76

PHILADELPHIA® 3-STEP® Toffee Crunch Cheesecake

Prep: 10 minutes plus refrigerating	*Bake:* 40 minutes

> 2 pkg. (8 oz. each) PHILADELPHIA Cream Cheese, softened
> ½ cup firmly packed brown sugar
> ½ tsp. vanilla
> 2 eggs
> 4 pkg. (1.4 oz. each) chocolate-covered English toffee bars, chopped (1 cup), divided
> 1 ready-to-use graham cracker crumb crust (6 oz. or 9 inch)

MIX cream cheese, sugar and vanilla with electric mixer on medium speed until well blended. Add eggs; mix until blended. Stir in ¾ cup of the chopped toffee bars.

POUR into crust. Sprinkle with remaining toffee bars.

BAKE at 350°F for 35 to 40 minutes or until center is almost set. Cool. Refrigerate 3 hours or overnight.   *Makes 8 servings*

Tip

Make Your Own Crust: *Mix 1⅓ cups graham cracker crumbs, 3 Tbsp. sugar and ⅓ cup butter or margarine, melted. Firmly press onto bottom and up side of 9-inch pie plate. Pour cheesecake batter into unbaked crust.*

PHILADELPHIA® 3-STEP® Pumpkin Layer Cheesecake

Prep: 10 minutes plus refrigerating	*Bake:* 40 minutes

> 2 pkg. (8 oz. each) PHILADELPHIA Cream Cheese, softened
> ½ cup sugar
> ½ tsp. vanilla
> 2 eggs
> ½ cup canned pumpkin
> ½ tsp. ground cinnamon
> Dash <u>each</u> ground cloves and nutmeg
> 1 ready-to-use graham cracker crumb crust (6 oz. or 9 inch)

MIX cream cheese, sugar and vanilla with electric mixer on medium speed until well blended. Add eggs; mix until blended.

STIR pumpkin and spices into 1 cup of the batter; pour remaining plain batter into crust. Top with pumpkin batter.

BAKE at 350°F for 35 to 40 minutes or until center is almost set. Cool. Refrigerate 3 hours or overnight. Store leftover cheesecake in refrigerator. *Makes 8 servings*

Holiday Cheesecake Presents

Prep: 10 minutes plus refrigerating	*Bake:* 30 minutes

1½ cups graham cracker crumbs
⅓ cup butter <u>or</u> margarine, melted
3 Tbsp. sugar
3 pkg. (8 oz. each) PHILADELPHIA Cream Cheese, softened
¾ cup sugar
1 tsp. vanilla
3 eggs

MIX crumbs, butter and 3 Tbsp. sugar; press onto bottom of 13×9-inch baking pan.

MIX cream cheese, ¾ cup sugar and vanilla with electric mixer on medium speed until well blended. Add eggs; mix until blended. Pour over crust.

BAKE at 350°F for 30 minutes or until center is almost set. Cool. Refrigerate 3 hours or overnight. Cut into bars. Decorate bars with decorating gels and sprinkles to resemble presents. Store leftover bars in refrigerator.   *Makes 2 dozen*

PHILADELPHIA® Snowmen Cookies

Prep: 20 minutes   *Bake:* 21 minutes

> 1 pkg. (8 oz.) PHILADELPHIA Cream Cheese, softened
> 1 cup powdered sugar
> ¾ cup (1½ sticks) butter <u>or</u> margarine
> ½ tsp. vanilla
> 2¼ cups flour
> ½ tsp. baking soda
>   Sifted powdered sugar
>   Miniature peanut butter cups (optional)

MIX cream cheese, 1 cup sugar, butter and vanilla with electric mixer on medium speed until well blended. Add flour and baking soda; mix well.

SHAPE dough into equal number of ½-inch and 1-inch diameter balls. Using 1 small and 1 large ball for each snowman, place balls, slightly overlapping, on ungreased cookie sheets. Flatten to ¼-inch thickness with bottom of glass dipped in additional flour. Repeat with remaining balls.

BAKE at 325°F for 19 to 21 minutes or until light golden brown. Cool on wire racks. Sprinkle each snowman with sifted powdered sugar. Decorate with icing as desired. Cut peanut butter cups in half for hats.   *Makes about 3 dozen*

PHILADELPHIA® Snowmen Cookies

Banana Split Cheesecake Squares

Prep: 20 minutes plus refrigerating   *Bake:* 30 minutes

Crust
  2 cups graham cracker crumbs
  ⅓ cup butter <u>or</u> margarine, melted
  ¼ cup sugar

Filling
  3 pkg. (8 oz. each) PHILADELPHIA Cream Cheese, softened
  ¾ cup sugar
  1 tsp. vanilla
  3 eggs
  ½ cup mashed ripe banana

Topping
  1 banana, sliced
  1 tsp. lemon juice
  1 cup halved strawberries
  1 can (8 oz.) pineapple chunks, drained
  Chopped nuts (optional)
  BAKER'S Semi-Sweet Baking Chocolate, melted (optional)

Crust
MIX crumbs, butter and sugar. Press onto bottom of 13×9-inch baking pan.

Filling
MIX cream cheese, sugar and vanilla with electric mixer on medium speed until well blended. Add eggs; mix until blended. Stir in mashed banana. Pour over crust. Bake at 350°F for 30 minutes or until center is almost set. Cool. Refrigerate 3 hours or overnight.

Topping
TOSS banana with lemon juice. Mix in strawberries and pineapple. Spoon evenly over cheesecake. Sprinkle with nuts and drizzle with chocolate. Cut into squares. Refrigerate any leftover cheesecake.

Makes 2 dozen

84

Shortbread Cookies

Prep: 15 minutes	*Bake:* 13 minutes

1½ cups (3 sticks) butter <u>or</u> margarine, softened
1 pkg. (8 oz.) PHILADELPHIA Cream Cheese, softened
½ cup granulated sugar
3 cups flour
Powdered sugar

MIX butter, cream cheese and granulated sugar until well blended.
Mix in flour.

SHAPE dough into 1-inch balls; place on ungreased cookie sheets.

BAKE at 400°F for 10 to 13 minutes or until light golden brown and
set; cool on wire racks. Sprinkle with powdered sugar.

Makes about 6 dozen

Variation

Holiday Cookies: *Tint dough with a few drops of food
coloring before shaping to add a festive touch.*

Frosted Pumpkin Squares

Prep: 20 minutes   *Bake:* 35 minutes

Cake
- ¾ cup (1½ sticks) butter <u>or</u> margarine
- 2 cups granulated sugar
- 1 can (16 oz.) pumpkin
- 4 eggs
- 2 cups flour
- 2 tsp. CALUMET Baking Powder
- 1 tsp. ground cinnamon
- ½ tsp. baking soda
- ½ tsp. salt
- ¼ tsp. ground nutmeg
- 1 cup chopped walnuts

Frosting
- 1 pkg. (8 oz.) PHILADELPHIA Cream Cheese, softened
- ⅓ cup butter <u>or</u> margarine
- 1 tsp. vanilla
- 3 cups sifted powdered sugar

Cake

MIX butter and sugar with electric mixer on medium speed until light and fluffy. Blend in pumpkin and eggs. Mix in combined dry ingredients. Stir in walnuts.

SPREAD into greased and floured 15×10×1-inch baking pan.

BAKE at 350°F for 30 to 35 minutes or until wooden pick inserted in center comes out clean; cool.

Frosting

MIX cream cheese, butter and vanilla in large bowl with electric mixer until creamy. Gradually add sugar, mixing well after each addition. Spread onto cake. Cut into squares.   *Makes 2 dozen*

Frosted Pumpkin Squares

Creamy Lemon Bars

Prep: 15 minutes   *Bake:* 35 minutes

1 pkg. (2-layer size) lemon cake mix
3 large eggs, divided
½ cup oil
2 pkg. (8 oz. each) PHILADELPHIA Cream Cheese, softened
1 container (8 oz.) BREAKSTONE'S <u>or</u> KNUDSEN Sour Cream
½ cup granulated sugar
1 tsp. grated lemon peel
1 Tbsp. lemon juice
Powdered sugar

MIX cake mix, 1 egg and oil. Press mixture onto bottom and up sides of lightly greased 15×10×1-inch baking pan. Bake at 350°F for 10 minutes.

MIX cream cheese with electric mixer on medium speed until smooth. Add remaining 2 eggs, sour cream, granulated sugar, peel and juice; mix until blended. Pour batter into crust.

BAKE at 350°F for 30 to 35 minutes or until filling is just set in center and edges are light golden brown. Cool. Sprinkle with powdered sugar. Cut into bars. Store leftover bars in refrigerator.

Makes 2 dozen

Creamy Lemon Bars

PHILADELPHIA® Cheesecake Brownies

Prep: 20 minutes	*Bake:* 40 minutes

1 pkg. (19.8 oz.) brownie mix (do not use mix that includes
   syrup pouch)
1 pkg. (8 oz.) PHILADELPHIA Cream Cheese, softened
⅓ cup sugar
1 egg
½ tsp. vanilla

PREPARE brownie mix as directed on package. Pour into greased
13×9-inch baking pan.

MIX cream cheese with electric mixer on medium speed until
smooth. Mix in sugar until blended. Add egg and vanilla; mix just
until blended. Pour cream cheese mixture over brownie batter; cut
through batter with knife several times for marble effect.

BAKE at 350°F for 35 to 40 minutes or until cream cheese mixture is
lightly browned. Cool. Cut into squares.   *Makes 2 dozen*

PHILADELPHIA® Cheesecake Brownies

PHILADELPHIA® Sugar Cookies

Prep: 10 minutes plus refrigerating	*Bake:* 15 minutes

---

1 pkg. (8 oz.) PHILADELPHIA Cream Cheese, softened
1 cup (2 sticks) butter <u>or</u> margarine, softened
⅔ cup sugar
¼ tsp. vanilla
2 cups flour
    Colored sugar, sprinkles and colored gels

MIX cream cheese, butter, ⅔ cup sugar and vanilla with electric mixer on medium speed until well blended. Mix in flour. Refrigerate several hours or overnight.

ROLL dough to ¼-inch thickness on lightly floured surface. Cut into desired shapes; sprinkle with colored sugar. Place on ungreased cookie sheets.

BAKE at 350°F for 12 to 15 minutes or until edges are lightly browned. Cool on wire racks. Decorate as desired with colored sugar, sprinkles and colored gels.   *Makes about 3½ dozen*